American Scream

Mark Evans

Copyright © 2016 Mark Evans

All rights reserved.

No portion of this book may be reproduced in any manner whatsoever without written permission from the author, except for brief excerpts for review purpose.

Format, Cover Design, Publisher:

Bill Boudreau, www.billboudreau.com

American Scream – Mark Evans

Table of Contents

1-Bicycle Summer 5
2-the green years up 6
3-First Car 7
4-Kennedy's Smile 8
5-Encapsulated 8
6-Cronus's Regret 10
7-Art Scavengers 11
8-Moving the Herd 12
9-News Room Massage Parlor 12
10-Break Room 14
11-Master of Fate 15
12-Medication Nation 16
14-ocracies and isms 17
13-American Scream 18
15-Street Poet 20
16-Medals 21
17-Poverty Equals Freedom 22
18-Phone Company 23
19-The Wall Street Blues 24
20-Borders 25
21-Single parent 26
22-The cow 27
23-Invitation to Anarchy 28
24-Beggars 29

25-Predatory Dreams 29
26-Shop 30
21st Century Dogs 31
28-Pope the President 32
29-Late Night Laundromat 33
30-Dropping Out 34
About the Author 36

1-Bicycle Summer

Cool wind in my ears
On my face
Knees and blood pump
Sweet sweat of youth
On a summer day I
Cut parking lot corners
Jump curbs, race my reflection
In store front windows
And go where cars can't.

Cut behind the Safeway
In the concrete shade of the loading dock
Through an Evil Knievel obstacle course
Of milk crates and pop bottles
Down the alley's quilted strip
Of shadow and light
Filtered through broad mimosa branches.

Their pink ballerinas dance while I
Peddle break neck speed
Through the open gate
The bike, riderless, rolls
To a stop and collapses
In thick Bermuda and
I'm already to the top
Of the back porch steps,
Pop is in the refrigerator,
And school and work and banks and wars
Are an eternity away.

2-the green years up

Robin and Sue

with their hair blown back

in the black convertible

leave their tracks on the asphalt streets

in the twilight gray

of a warm summer night

they breathe bathing suits and boys and bare feet

and somewhere in the distance

along the horizon

a siren screams hot-blooded-hell of sorrow

but they do not hear.

They swing from the green years

And fly naked into the middle of the river

3-First Car

My son talks about automobiles,
sports cars and luxury and convertibles,
(it's okay for him to dream)
he says all he wants is his own set of wheels
(the convertible is preferable),
he says a car will make him more responsible,
but I know what he wants. . .I remember:

He wants to drag main late on a summer night
with one arm draped across the steering wheel
and the other hanging loose out the window;
he wants to talk to girls in their cars at stoplights;
he wants to look through his windshield
at a night so fresh
that everything is happening for the first time,
and he wants to swing from a rope
and land in the front seat of a convertible . . .
that his father helped him buy.

I remember . . .and I want to drag main again,
and I want to talk to girls at stoplights
(without talking to the police),
and I want to see summer nights
as if they are new,
and I want to swing from a rope . . .
without hurting my back.

And now I know how *my* father felt,
long ago when I still itched with anticipation,
when I was full of confidence which could not
fail. He had envy, not anger in his eyes,
when he tossed me the keys and said, "Boy.
don't make me have to bail you out of jail."

4-Kennedy's Smile

John F. Kennedy
knew how to smile
as smooth and broad
as the curve of Cape Cod
with sandy hair and fair cheeks
and white Mt. Rushmore teeth.
He smiled with his eyes
in a relaxed, casual style
and, once, he had smiled sheepishly
at a less than innocent,
"Happy birthday, Mr. President"
and that had made everyone smile
to see him squirm
and act like a regular guy.
Yes
John F. Kennedy smiled a lot
and that's what he was doing
smiling and waving
the moment before he was shot.

5-Encapsulated

Encapsulated
(wanna break these chains)
Got the stress syndrome
(swirlin' down the drain)
Isolated
(can't hear myself think)
Lookin for a home
(there's blood in the sink)

American Scream – Mark Evans

Dependency
(I'm superman)
Intimacy
(I'm superman)
Masculinity
(I'm superman)
Honesty
(believe me if you can)

Incarcerated
(wanna break these chains)
Company man
(swirlin down the drain)
Dominated
(can't hear myself think)
Shit hits the fan
(there's blood in the sink)

Full of doubt
(I'm every man)
Clumsy lout
(I'm every man)
Toss me out
(I'm every man)
You have to shout
(I'm every man)

Just hit me in the mouth
Just hit me in the mouth
Just hit me in the mouth
And make me bleed.

6-Cronus's Regret

nuclear childhood
irradiated snow ice-cream
tv dinners and "Gunsmoke"
(it's only a flesh wound)
before bedtime and the
missile and mushroom cloud dreams.
("and now a word from our sponsors")
a rip in social curtain reveals
the monster, gagging, a sick god
bloated on his own children
(canned laughter, fake blood)
rifle in a warehouse window
riots and war from the tv screen
fire-hose foam of hands and feet
police batons and blood in the street
(stay tuned for the Great Society
coming soon to a neighborhood near you)

years later fears remain
conscience cannot come clean

7-Art Scavengers

Shopping cart
Click click clicks
Down the white tile isle
`Past the cereal splash Jack
Son Pollock painting in
The corner of my eye
I resist the urge for sugar
And click my cart to the
Red meat counter where
Steaks are arranged like Picasso's bull
In rectangular beds of Styrofoam and cellophane
A woman in a dark coat eyes a slab of ribs
I lean over the ground beef and pick through packages
Like an old crow.

8-Moving the Herd

whips snap, sharp barks,
men and dogs
bring terror.
desperation pushes back,
the herd churns earth,
fights itself to avoid a greater fear,
panic is electric
mass of muscle strains to escape,
necks stretch, wild eyes roll, look to the sky.

Picasso's bull has been broken.
terror has found direction.
the flow, under control,
pools like water
behind a dam and spurts in a steady stream
through the loading chute.

9-News Room Massage Parlor

Massage my brain with
Fashion model anchors, and
Seductive reports of terror (tied down,
Gaged and helpless, can't look away),
Velvet voiced, the evening
Dose of fear is delivered quietly to the client
Small increments dig deep
Into the muscles of memory ("how does that feel?
There is no safe word.") sandwiched between
Two minutes of commercial dreams of the
American Dream of the perfect
Family of the perfect car and the
Perfect smiles, followed by the joy of

American Scream – Mark Evans

Anti-depressant medication
("Cut. That's a take.")

Press down on me until my
Spine pops with catastrophes of
War and far off refugees
And remind me that it could be worse.
The pain could be real.
I can still stand up and walk away, but
Dig your thumbs of numbing news
Into my frontal lobe, probe
And knead until soft and pliable
Karate chop and tenderize and
Leave me with a happy ending of
Human interest that makes me smile and cry.
Fade out with, "Good night, and stay tuned for
The Price is Right."

My media dominatrix
Massages me with pain, sentiment and sorrow.
I'll be back again tomorrow.

10-Break Room

Sit at the table
By the vending machine.
A short line
Of people wait
To plug it with quarters.
A white face hangs
On a yellow wall
Above the coffee pot.
"Tick tock," around and around
The second hand moves silently.
No matter.
I hear it from where I sit,
Calling me back.
My reflection
Floats face up.
I Look myself in the eye,
Drink the cup dry,
And I'm gone, gone, gone.

11-Master of Fate

I built pyramids for pharaohs,
Roads for Caesar,
Castles for feudal kings,
Forged steel for Andrew Carnegie,
And for Henry, I assembled the Model T.
They stood on my shoulders
And claimed to be the masters of their destiny.

I mined the coal, ruff necked oil,
Built the houses, plowed the soil
To put a meal on my plate,
Pulled the cotton, hoed the rows,
Sold everything but my soul,
Weathered droughts, dust bowls, hurricanes . . .
My master has become the company store,
And I hang each month at the end of my rope
Facing financial disaster . . . .
I survive. I always do.
But the children lose hope and
The old die faster.

I am a name and a face soon forgotten.
I am turnips and potatoes.
I am the man whose shoulders ache
From carrying someone else's gold.

I don't know how much more I can take.
But know this:
If I stumble and fall, so will all who say
That they are the masters of their fate.

12-Medication Nation

We don't know the cause
Of your illness, if it is
Malignant or benign,
Nerve, organ, muscle,
If it's physical at all . . .
Perhaps the problem is in your mind.
Don't worry; we have something
To help you unwind.
Lower back pain,
Morning migraine,
Anxiety, depression,
Sinus membrane infection. . .
Whatever your malady,
We provide a remedy
A pharmaceutical solution,
Just ask your family MD
(or if normal is how you feel,
speed dial your main man and make a deal).

We're a medication nation
and we're feeling no pain
for health or recreation
the answer is the same.

Warning: may cause constipation, vomiting,
ringing in the ears,
hallucinations, addiction, heart palpitations,
Discontinue use if a rash appears
or thoughts of suicide occur.

Those who survive the medication
have an excellent chance of being cured.

14-ocracies and isms

Ocracies and isms
are all invisible prisons,
hand-cuffed with a Rolex or
bound by an hourly wage,
rush hour, lunch hour, happy hour
march through the yard each day.

we manufacture ruts
in our work week cells,
retire each night
rewarded by consumables
and dreams of higher wages,
and we volunteer gladly
to lock our own cages.

13-American Scream

Marble headed from the
Weight of working until happy hour
Chase the week with a case of
Canned alcohol and canned laughter . . .

The next morning:
Cartoons, commercials, and
General Mills processed wheat breakfast
Action figures kick ass
While dad and mom dream of diving
Into ("Zero interest
Or 1,000 dollars back")
New cars driven by happy
Actors across a television screen

Download Beauty from photo shop
Face book profile
A thousand friends and no one speaks, but

The right shampoo will change your life

Back at work . . .
Break room gossip
Bulimic receptionist
Alcoholic boss
Xanax from Frank on the loading dock

("Discontinue use if thoughts of suicide occur")

Punch the clock at 5
Not a minute early
Drive through for fast food
Super models in bathing suits

American Scream – Mark Evans

Say girls go wild for
light beer and a fluoride smile

Fantasies at the stop light
(. . . truck is just a prop
. . . working undercover . . . much more than
what I seem)
Food wrappers on the floorboard
Hand gun in the glove box

Living the latest version
Of the American Dream

15-Street Poet

It don't take much to be a street poet.
Just a few scars from the neighborhood
And a few words to show you know it.
Know the hopelessness, that is,
Of cramped quarters and wafer thin walls
And project hallways late at night
Where the doors all open to strangers.

It don't take much to be a street poet.
Just some bad teeth and some bad habits
And a few bad words to show you know it.
That is, know where hope is cut into dimes
And sold in the shadows to the hopeless,
Who will be back tomorrow for more,
Where white snow turns to gray slush
in the gutters.

It don't take much to be a street poet.
Just some wild eyes and nappy hair
And a few crazy words to show you know it.
Know how to survive, that is,
How to squeeze like a weed
Through the concrete cracks,
To sprout between empty bottles of cheap wine,
And bloom into a brilliant sun
In the ragged back alleys of the mind

It don't take much.

16-Medals

As a child, I found the medals
In their slim black cases,
Buried deep in a dresser drawer.
But he only shook his head
And put them back.
He carried a deep scar
Across one shoulder.
Whenever I asked,
He would change the subject.
I understood, as I grew older,
And stopped asking.
His silence had told me all I needed to know.

17-Poverty Equals Freedom

Poverty . . .
Equals . . .
Freedom . . .
the projects
Equals
Freedom
inner city schools
Equals
Freedom
minimum wage jobs
Equals
Freedom
hopes put on hold
Equals
Freedom
hustlin' to survive
Equals
Freedom
low expectations
Equals
Freedom
dreams left behind.
Equals . . . Freedom . . . .

18-Phone Company

3G, 4G must have technology
satellite out of sight
broad band at my command
status statement
monthly payment
around my neck
in my ear
let me text
let me hear
clear connection
wide selection
information
date and time
streaming music
videos, pictures
(you show me yours
and I'll show you mine)
fashion trends
family and friends
work networks
in my car
my backyard
at the baseball game
browsing through
the grocery store
can't ignore
the symphonic score
of my personalized
ring-tone

cell phone . . .
never alone.

19-The Wall Street Blues

it's a hard, hard life . . .
when my worth depends
on the dollar, the pound, the euro, and yen
on supply and demand
for corn and rice
on a barrel of oil's
fluctuating price
it's a hard, hard life . . .

when the market falls
and depression comes
and my dividends end
tax hikes for the wealthy
portfolio's unhealthy
and Bernie Madoff is my friend
it's a hard, hard life . . .

when congress calls
and I plead the fifth
because I've already told lies,
when I short my own clients
I hope they'll understand
it's only free enterprise, and
it's a hard, hard life . . .

when I foreclose Detroit
and invest in Bejing
to pad my bottom line
it's a sacrifice that I must make
if I want to retire before I turn 39
it's a hard, hard life . . .

Lord knows workin' Wall Street ain't easy.

20-Borders

I cannot see the borders
that make the shapes of countries
and keep people apart,
though on the map those lines are clearly drawn.
I expect to see something more
ominous and foreboding . . .
Like the line separating good and evil . . .
More than the middle aged crossing guards
and customs clerks who greet me.
Beyond the checkpoints and fences
and signs and walls
I see only rivers and mountains and deserts and
towns and fields that look the same
on one side as the other.

No borders have been drawn
to mark where you end and I begin,
but eyes meet above the table at breakfast
or over a desk in an office at work,
and border guards come to attention, and
rivers and deserts and mountain ranges
divide into *yours* and *mine*
and invisible lines
keep us isolated and alone
in a crowded world.

21-Single parent

I expected to
enjoy my food more,
after all the I do's and do I's
and becauses and whys,
after eating meals between
diapers and PTA meetings
and band and baseball practices
I thought the taste of my food
would linger longer.
after years of drive through and microwaves
and dinner on the run for three instead of one,
I looked forward to digestion with relaxation.

those frantic family meals are gone.
now, I eat alone.

22-The cow

Stares stupidly from behind the fence
Chewing, chewing, chewing
Then pissing . . .

Ancient cattle were
Quick and lean and tall
Their wild spirits roamed the plains
Captured and tamed
Only in paintings on dark cave walls
Unlike our thick cows that stand
Like clay statues
Their days dumb with redundancy
In fenced green fields of hay

How the cow has evolved!
From a dangerous storm
Of horns and hooves
To a sluggish quadrupod,
Fed and fat and led
From the feeding trough
To the slaughter house without a thought.

Beware how the cow has evolved.

23-Invitation to Anarchy

Throw away your rings
they just get stuck on knuckles
don't answer the phone
but if you must speak in tongues
dismantle all boxes
use rule books to start campfires

(get in line dot your i's pay your fines
shoe your shines tie your ties
you're 5 minutes late payment is due
I do I do I do not walk across in the middle of the
block only at the corners red. means. stop.
green means go no matter what. . .)

smile and sing happy songs
at funerals and other family functions
and go skinny dipping
at midnight when you're sixty
in cool rivers of Now
naked at night under the stars. . .
and for no good reason chuckle
and throw away your rings. . .
they just get stuck on knuckles.

24-Beggars

He takes his place
Sitting at the base
Of a stoplight pole
In a busy intersection.
His cardboard sign says
"please help God bless"
And his hair is a mess
From a night under the bridge, but
The stray pup beside him
Lends a sense of dignity
And completes the
Red light hierarchy of
Pup . . .
Man on the curb . . .
Woman in the car with windows rolled up.

25-Predatory Dreams

I dreamed
I ran in a herd
of predators,
big cats and wolves and
sheep with neck ties
and glock 9's and 40 hour work weeks,
and we ate each other alive, a little at a time.
Then I woke . . . .

26-Shop

shop shop
parking lot slot
rectangular plot
points toward
a massive mouth open wide
consumes consumers
promises savings inside
lowest prices of the year
and other rumors of
good will to men
and a guy dressed in red rings a bell
beside plastic reindeer (20% off Holiday Sale)

shopping cart
empty heart
waits to be filled
taps the tile with each step
a problem with the wheel
its presence announced at every isle
click click click feels its way
through the maze
frustrated rat in a fluorescent cage
drop the minimum wage into the cart
fill that heart with Christmas cheer
proceed to the next available cashier
hum along with the intercom
"all is calm, all is bright . . ."
swipe the card out the door into the night

parking lot slot
rectangular plot

21st Century Dogs

21st Century dogs
more like sheep
than the wild wolves
we once were,
we chase our tails
and wear our woolen straightjackets
with matching slacks and neckties.
We have forgotten
the hunger of the hunt
the freedom of the full moon and
we find trails wherever we walk.

confined in our close cage
we snarl and bite
and wait for the bell to tell us
to move to another cubicle
and we no longer search
the tired boundaries
of our pen.

28-Pope the President

Pope the President
Congress the Courts
Flag the pledge
Pray the vote

Dollar the media
Market the stock
Channel the change
Punch the clock

Go to work
Daily bread
Tree sky stream flower
Poet the break rooms
People the power

29-Late Night Laundromat

Late at night at the Laundromat and
The rattle and squeak of children
Has faded with the sunset
Into the quiet murmur of machines,
And the air is heavy and sweet
With the scent of fabric
Clean and hot from the dryer.

A young couple, too new
To own a home machine,
Too much in love to care,
A universe unto themselves,
Smile over their clothes
All folded and tossed together
Into their basket of dreams.

Washing machines hum lullabies
In the late night Laundromat
Where stacks of magazines go to retire
Where no one really wants to speak
Where eyes don't meet
and people always look bored or tired. . .
Unless they are in love.

Outside, the street is empty, but
The sky is full of moon and stars.
They hover above a window of light,
An oasis in the heart of the night,
Where souls can go, in love or alone,
To wash away the stains of the day
And prepare for the next American dawn.

30-Dropping Out

Don't want to fill society's niche
or to be the target of a strategic market
or credit plans or a commercial sales pitch
and I no longer think of myself
as a cog in something turning.

Don't measure me
by an hourly wage and the car I own.
I want to walk everywhere I go.
I want to take my time and go there slow.
It's my time and I want to roll it around
in my mouth and taste it before I swallow.
I want something to remember
besides a full belly.

I'm tired of fast food
and the fast lane and fast fixes that
only make me want more of the same.
I'm tired of the television telling me
that people won't like me if I sweat
in an effort to persuade me to buy
the new improved deodorant.

I no longer pay attention
to the steady stream of messages
classic rock soundtracks and
computer enhanced graphics
designed to tell me who I am and what I need.
I'll stop my ears and sing my own songs.
I'll determine my identity and where I belong
and how I live my life.

American Scream – Mark Evans

Come on, let's go . . .
I've seen the scenery before . . .
Let's ditch the world of supply and demand.
Let's leave cardboard and plastic behind.
Don't want to be part of the program.
I'm taking a slow train
to a different state of mind.
Come on, let's go.

About the Author

Mark Evans is the single father of two sons, who are now men. He received a Master's of Art in Education from the University of Central Oklahoma. He has worked as a public school teacher, as a freelance writer with B. B. and E. editorial service, as a writer/editor for Economy Publishing Co., and at numerous part-time jobs. He would rather not give any more information about himself, saying, "I'm more interesting when people don't know me."

Made in the USA
San Bernardino, CA
16 March 2016